JOHN FITZGERALD KENNEDY
THE WORLD REMEMBERS

JOHN FITZGERALD KENNEDY
THE WORLD REMEMBERS

by Alex J. Goldman

ℭℱ

FLEET PRESS CORPORATION

New York

Frontispiece: A woman of West Berlin at the ceremony dedicating
a memorial plaque to John Fitzgerald Kennedy

HOMAGE IN SILENCE

Foreword

"Tributes only emphasize our loss." said former President Harry S. Truman when he dedicated the home of Franklin Delano Roosevelt as a national shrine. He struck the keynote of the profound meaning of memorials.

Each country was acting individually, seeking its own means of expression to perpetuate the name and image of John Fitzgerald Kennedy.

Memorials to his name dot the globe. Not all are massive or elaborately adorned, but they express the deep desire of the peoples of the world to preserve the memory. Recorded here are some of these tributes, conceived or executed.

Many countries have dedicated educational and cultural ventures to honor his name. Streets throughout the world, from Montreal, Canada, to Kigali, Rwanda, are known by the name of Kennedy. Special awards have been created for those who have distinguished themselves in fields perpetuating the ideals and spirit of the late President. Libraries and institutions carry his name. Mountains in Canada and in Italy have been renamed in his honor as well as numerous airports, waterworks, and bridges.

To all of these memorials must be added the countless commemorative medals and stamps issued which testify to the magnetism of his name.

Although it was not possible in one volume to include all of the world dedications, I humbly accept the challenge of the task of up-dating this volume in the future, for these are only the beginning of the countless remembrances to this fallen hero.

The tragedy of his death was felt by all. This perhaps is his greatest memorial.

Alex J. Goldman

Stamford, Connecticut
September, 1968

Acknowledgments

Perhaps the greatest reward in preparing this volume came from the many people I have met in government and private organizations and the extensive correspondence with so many cooperative embassies of countries affiliated with the United Nations.

I am deeply grateful to the many individuals representing news bureaus and governmental agencies who were most generous in providing many rich sources of information.

These acknowledgments would not be complete without special thanks to:

E. A. Comee, Agency for International Development, Department of State; Fernando Demaria, Estancia, *La Sarita,* La Pampa, Argentina; F. H. Rogan, Melbourne, Australia (Town Clerk); Bundeskanzlevant, Vienna, Austria; Dr. Otto A. Zundritsch, Director, Austrian Information Service, New York; Embassy of the Argentine Republic, Washington, D. C.; Mission Permanente de la Republique Gabonaise; Barbados Tourist Board, Washington, D. C.; Roger Vaurs, Director, Ambassade de France; Jean Beliard, Ministre Plenipotentiaire, Ambassade de France; Department des Affairs Culturellas et des Beux Arts, Liege, Belgium; O. P. Gabites, Consul General of New Zealand, New York; British Information Services, New York; R. L. Cameron, Department of Mines and Technical Surveys, Ottawa, Canada; Ministry of the Interior, Nicosia, Cyprus; Permanent Mission, United Nations, Republic of Cyprus; Claver Ryabonyende, Republique Rwandaise Mission Permanente; Chinese News Service, New York; Kaj Bruun, Danish Information Service, New York; The Kennedy Memorial Trust, London, England; Hadassah, Women's Zionist Organization, New York; T. C. Cheng, The John F. Kennedy Center, Hong Kong; The Red Cross, Hong Kong; Hugo Pascualy, Consulado General, Colombia; Dennis B. O'Sullivan, John Swift, and James Flavin, Consulate of Ireland, New York; Paul O'Dwyer and Martin Kileen, Irish Institute, New York; A. Berrah, Mission Permanente de la Republique de Cote d'Ivoire; Rabbis Philip Shneirson and Milton Aron, Jewish National Fund, New York; Susan Emery, John F. Kennedy Center for the Performing Arts, Washington, D. C.; J. K. Kimani, Ministry of Foreign Affairs, Nairobi, Kenya; Embassy of Korea, Washington, D. C.; Doo Yong Song, John F. Kennedy Memorial Hall, Tongduchon, Korea; Hon. Otto E. Passman, Congressman; Foreign Service of the United States, Bern Switzerland; Abdeslam Jaidi, Embassy of Morocco, Washington D. C.; National Geographic Society, Washington, D. C.; Embassy of Spain, Washington, D. C.; *The New York Times,* New York; Turkish Tourism and Information Center, New York; Royal Thai Embassy, Washington, D. C.; Amerigo Tot, Rome, Italy; Permanent Mission of the Yemen Arab Republic, New York; Bruno Herlitzka, Marlborough Galleria D'Arte, Rome, Italy; The *Daily American,* Rome, Italy; A. David Weisgal, American Committee for the Weizmann Institute of Sciences (in Israel), New York; German Information Center, New York; Embassy of Cambodia, Washington, D. C.; Mission Permanente du Cambodge Aupres de O'Organisative des National Unies; Ramo Ramovic, Bosnakolklor Company, Sarajevo, Yugoslavia; Edward C. Rochette, Krause Publications, Iola, Wisconsin, E. C. Rochette, American Numismatic Association, Colorado Springs, Colorado; Ulla Christiansen, Danish Information Office, New York; A. C. F. N. Jones, Association of Commonwealth Universities, London, England; Wolfgang Sievers, Melbourne, Australia; Direction de la Documentation, Paris, France; M. Appelmann, Burgermeister, Stadt Offenbach, a. M. West Germany.

Contents

JOHN FITZGERALD KENNEDY
THE WORLD REMEMBERS

COUNTRIES OF THE WORLD

Memorial at Quemu-Quemu, Argentina

ARGENTINA

"The man who despised danger, who made a cult of courage, who endowed with all the intellectual and material gifts that life can offer, and being President of the most powerful country in the world, he yet worried about the pressing needs of the weakest, John F. Kennedy has become our captain and guide in this stormy era. And he has obliged us to realize that his 'New Frontier' is no longer a theoretical formula. It has become a vital necessity for the peoples of all America. For the United States because it provides a challenge to its creative capacity and to its obligation to fulfill the revolution begun in Philadelphia in 1776; for Latin America because it contains a possibility of showing to all mankind that freedom and well-being can coexist.

"This is Kennedy's message and the legacy that the present generations have received. This is Kennedy's survival after his death.

"Here in the Pampa, where the limitless plains proclaim a future full of greatness, where the sky and the earth meet to form the unattainable horizon of ceaseless human progress, an imposing block of cement will raise its shape to the heights to show the wanderer that John F. Kennedy has triumphed in America because above all the vicissitudes that his ideals may undergo, the imprint of his life has left an indelible mark on the spirit of the American man."

So spoke Dr. Ismael Amit, Governor of La Pampa, Argentina, on September 21, 1964, at Quemu Quemu, 450 miles southwest of Buenos Aires. The imposing monument he referred to was one of the many memorials erected, and of streets and schools named in memory of the late President in this South American land about which President Kennedy had written on May 24, 1961, ". . .the United States and the cause of freedom has no stronger or more respected friends than the people of Argentina."

Argentina had responded swiftly to the news of the President's assassination. Almost immediately, Argentina issued a series of four postage stamps memorializing Kennedy, the first country in the world to do so.

The people of Argentina displayed their love and admiration as they planned the inspiring memorial. A special commission, consisting of the most distinguished officials and leaders of the Argentine, was selected to plan for an appropriate structure.

The Commission declared its purpose:

A genuine love animates the Pampa men and women who desire to perpetuate in stone their admiration for the great American President. On the earth, trod upon only by the plowshare, in the fertile pampa, on the infinite horizon, under the blue sky, beside our flag, tinged with glory, the wings of Kennedy will soar in eternal exaltation.

Landmark of human progress, the graceful lines that will honor his soul shall guide men toward the oasis, urging him to social enterprise, impelling him toward every field of excellence, in grace and concord.

Our symbol and starting point will be markers for all men of good will. . . .

Created by famed sculptor Lincoln Presno and a team of experts, including the architect Juan Jose Casal Rocco and engineers Julio Arigon and Lionel Vierra — all Uruguayans — they shared in the memorable creation as a labor of love.

ARGENTINA

The massive marble and granite monument, at the crossroads of Routes 1 and 12 in the municipality of Quemu-Quemu, in the province of the Pampa, was erected in the form of a marble rectangle 130 feet high, 40 feet wide, and 15 feet thick. It is set on a base of black granite. A tall, stylized triangular hole was hewn at the center of the rectangle. A triangular structure of marble, and of the same size and shape as the cut-out portion, was set horizontally across the base of the triangular hole, thus forming a kind of upside-down cross.

The space of the ascending triangle symbolizes the eternal and ascendant spirit of Kennedy, and the triangular descending prism of the recumbent representation of death. Together, they suggest the symbol of the cross.

The thirteen-story marble arch in the shape of the letter "A" was dedicated on May 29, 1967. United States Ambassador Edward M. Martin, speaking on behalf of the Kennedy family, said at the ceremonies:

> If the Alliance for Progress is a living monument to the memory of John F. Kennedy, then there is beginning here today, in the Pampa, a new monument which spells out the enduring admiration and affection he awakened in the Argentine people.

AUSTRALIA

Australia, called by some "the island continent," has memorialized President Kennedy.

In Melbourne, the City Council adopted the suggestion of the Lord Mayor of Melbourne, Sir Leon Curtis, for a memorial to the late President, and assigned an island in an ornamental lake in one of the city's many parks. This memorial, unveiled by the Lord Mayor on March 25, 1965, is a bronze bas-relief head, set on a seven-foot-high granite boulder and bearing the inscription: "John F. Kennedy 1917–1963."

A 17-foot bronze flagpole rises on the opposite side of the island.

At the entrance to the island, a plaque bears this inscription:

> This memorial signifies the grateful recognition by the Citizens of this City for the services given by John F. Kennedy as President of the United States of America, 1960–1963.

The bas-relief was done by Raymond Ewers, a Melbourne sculptor. A bridge, specially built, joins the island and the city.

Bas-relief memorial, Melbourne, Australia

John Fitzgerald Kennedy House, Vienna, Austria

AUSTRIA

A telegram signed "John F. Kennedy" was received by Dr. Heinrich Drimmel, Austria's Minister of Education, a few hours before the President's death. It was probably his last message. The telegram became, in effect, a memorial for two martyred Presidents, Abraham Lincoln and John F. Kennedy. A long-planned centennial commemoration of the Gettysburg Address had been scheduled for November 24, 1963.

On the brilliantly lighted and crowded stage of Vienna's Burgtheater, the director of the theater, Ernst Haeussermann, stepped slowly to the rostrum at the opening of the program and read these words from President Kennedy:

> Dear Mr. Drimmel: The inspiring idea which Lincoln so simply and movingly expressed in his Gettysburg Address has become the common heritage of all people throughout the world who cherish freedom and human dignity. These deathless words unite us and represent a force of magnificent spiritual strength in the world of today. Please accept my greetings and warmest wishes for your undertaking.

The *Egmont Overture* had been scheduled to open the festive event. In its stead, the Vienna Symphony Orchestra played the Funeral theme of the *Eroica* symphony in tribute to John Fitzgerald Kennedy.

"The people of Austria," President Kennedy had said on June 6, 1961, following his visit, "know what it is to live under occupation and they know what it is to live in freedom. . . ." They responded with profound shock at the news of the assassination. The state radio network was silenced for five minutes. Entertainment programs were cancelled or changed to fit the occasion. Churches held special services, flags were lowered.

One year later, on November 21, 1964, a solemn requiem mass was held in memory of John F. Kennedy in the Vienna Franziskaner Church. The service, "Requiem in Anniversario," including Mozart's *Requiem* was performed by the Akademia-Kammerchor.

The most prominent Austrian memorial is the Kennedy Bridge in Vienna. The Hietzig Bridge, across the River Wien, which President Kennedy crossed in June, 1961, for talks with Premier Khrushchev, was formally opened after complete modernization, on September 11, 1964. It stands near the villa of the United States Ambassador, where President and Mrs. Kennedy stayed and where the President entertained Khrushchev at luncheon.

Austria also boasts the John F. Kennedy Hof, a private undertaking of a building association, the Verein der Freunde des Wohnungseigentums. It is one of Vienna's most beautiful new apartment buildings, located in the Rotenturmstrasse, in the center of town.

The builders of the modern eight-story structure wanted to commemorate Kennedy's relentless fight for the freedom of all peoples throughout the world. The proximity of the building to the heart of Austrian Catholicism — the Gothic St. Stephans Cathedral and the Archbishop's residence just across the street, was deemed appropriate in memory of Kennedy's faith. The John F. Kennedy Hof stands on a site whose history can be traced back to the fourteenth century when imperial councilors, rich tradesmen, and titled nobility lived on one of the most select sites of the city.

The unveiling of a John F. Kennedy memorial plaque highlighted the dedication on December 19, 1964. Dr. Josef Klaus, Austrian Chancellor, delivered the principal address and James A. Riddleberger, United States Ambassador, responded.

The consecration and blessing of the house was presided over by Franz Cardinal Koenig.

Kennedy Bridge, Vienna, Austria

Kennedy Bridge, Vienna, Austria

John Fitzgerald Kennedy House, Vienna, Austria

John Fitzgerald Kennedy Bridge, Pont Neuf, Liege, Belgium

BELGIUM

In his toast to Prince Albert of Belgium, February 26, 1963, President Kennedy said:

> . . . We value the friendship between Belgium and the United States, which is an old one. . .

A similar theme was reflected in the address of Bourgemeister M. Maurice Destenay, January 4, 1964, offering a resolution to the City Council of Liege, suggesting that the new bridge be dedicated to the name of John Fitzgerald Kennedy.

He stated that the city of Liege modestly yet fervently inaugurates the new year by dedicating the Pont Neuf to the memory of the fallen President and the mission to which he had believed in during his life.

BRAZIL

In July, 1961, President Kennedy said:

"No area in this hemisphere is in greater or more urgent need of attention than Brazil's vast Northeast. . . . This area with its poverty, hunger, and consequent discontent is a crucible of social, economic and political problems — problems which have unmistakable implications for the future development of Brazil and the security of the entire hemisphere. . . . And the United States intends to play a continuing role in helping our sister Republic of Brazil meet this urgent challenge. . ."

The Vila Kennedy Project is one of a number of efforts begun by the State of Guanabara to attack the serious urban housing problem in Rio de Janeiro, where 800,000 people lead precarious, unhygienic lives as squatters in hillside slum communities (*favelas*).

Built in cooperation with the Agency for International Development of the Department of State under the Alliance for Progress, a notable feature of this pilot housing project was the arrangement whereby federal, state, and local governments for the first time pooled their financial resources in planning and executing a housing development.

The state of Guanabara is building and improving upon the Vila Kennedy experience and is continuing similar low-cost housing construction on a sizeable scale in the Rio metropolitan area.

AID projects bearing the Kennedy name are generally so designated at the request of the host country. Brazil requested this honor for the late President.

Vila Kennedy, Rio de Janeiro, Brazil

La Belle Avenue J. F. Kennedy, Sihanoukville, Cambodia

CAMBODIA

The second largest city of Cambodia, Sihanoukville, named after Prince Norodom Sihanouk, was the scene of ceremonies naming an avenue after the late President. Pnompenh is the chief city of this land in the Indochina area of Southeast Asia.

On November 6, 1967, Mrs. Jacqueline Kennedy and her party, including Lord Harlech, former British Ambassador to the United States, Charles Bartlett, newspaper columnist and his wife, and Michael Forrestal, New York attorney and former White House aide, flew into Sihanoukville for the dedicatory rites. They had spent three days visiting the famous ruins of Angkor, capital of the ancient Khmers Empire which ruled Southeast Asia from the 700's to the 1400's.

The Prince, speaking of the memorial, stressed that it was "a modest avenue that at least in our eyes seems unworthy of the illustrious man of state whose name it carries."

Mrs. Kennedy, accompanying Prince Sihanouk across a red carpet to unveil a plaque containing the name of the avenue, responded by saying that her late husband had planned to write an address on the theme of the ancient vision of "peace on earth and good will toward all men," and she expressed the hope that the avenue bearing his name would remind all who pass this way of the ancient vision of which he spoke.

The 2 1/2-mile avenue known in Cambodia as "La Belle Avenue J. F. Kennedy" commences at the famous Lions of Cambodia project and concludes its passageway at the O Chhoeuteal, where rises the official residence of the Chief of State.

Sihanoukville, Cambodia

Sihanoukville, Cambodia

CANADA

The tallest memorial on earth to John F. Kennedy stands majestically and enchantingly "as lone as God and white as a winter's moon" in nature's captivating beauty, where, in President Kennedy's words. . . "Geography has made us neighbors. History has made us friends. Economics has made us partners. And necessity has made us allies. Those whom nature hath so joined together, let no man put asunder."*

It is a mountain peak in the Yukon, a northward extension of the Cordillera, the western highlands of North America, close to the international boundary, enduring in this way as a symbol of friendship of the two great nations of northern North America.

The Yukon — a land of mountain-fringed plateau and broad, parklike valleys — occupies the extreme northwestern part of Canada. This is more than twice the size of Great Britain and nearly as large as the four Atlantic provinces combined.

Mount Kennedy, 13,900 feet high, jutting sharply heavenward, was discovered in 1935 by Dr. Bradford Washburn, Director of the Museum of Science, Boston, Massachusetts, who at twenty four years of age led the Yukon Exhibition for the National Geographic Society. It joins a number of other ice-capped peaks in the St. Elias Range, where Mount Logan towers 19,850

*May 17, 1961, address before the Canadian Parliament.

◄§ 36

Mount Kennedy, The Yukon, Canada

Mount Kennedy, The Yukon, Canada

feet, second on the continent only to Mount McKinley in Alaska. In the same range are: Mount St. Elias, 18,008 feet, Mount Luciania, 17,150 feet, Mount Steele, 16,439 feet, Mount Wood, 15,880 feet, Mount Vancouver, 15,720 feet, Mount Walsh, 14,780 feet, and Mount Craig, 13,250 feet. Mount Kennedy's nearest neighbor is Mount Hubbard, 14,950 feet, named for Gardiner Greene Hubbard, first president of the National Geographic Society.

CANADA

The first person ever to scale and land on Mount Kennedy, after the peak was officially named by Prime Minister Lester B. Pearson in January, 1965, was the President's brother, the late Senator, Robert F. Kennedy.

On March 24, 1965, the Yukon Expedition was led once again by Dr. Washburn for the National Geographic Society. Robert Kennedy reached the summit, until then the highest unclimbed mountain in North America — and afterward described his experience in these words:

> Mount Kennedy is a magnificent mountain — lonely, stark, forbidding. The utter desolation of that part of the Yukon Territory only emphasizes the peak's beauty. . . .
>
> President Kennedy loved the outdoors. He loved adventure. He admired courage more than any other human quality, and he was President of the United States, which is frequently and accurately called the lonliest job in the world.
>
> So I am sure he would be pleased that this lonely, beautiful mountain in the Yukon bears his name, and that in this way, at least, he has joined the fraternity of those who live outdoors, battle the elements, and climb mountains.*

Atop the mountain, Senator Kennedy planted a black-bordered flag with the family crest or coat-of-arms — three gold helmets on a black background, in his brother's memory.

National Geographic Magazine, July, 1965.

Senator Kennedy was a member of three teams that attempted the slow and dangerous ascent. It took some five hours from Camp 2, which is 3,000 feet from the base. He was part of a three-man team which included James W. Whittaker of Seattle, Washington, who, in 1963, became the first American to scale Mt. Everest. The third man was Barry W. Pratker of Tacoma, Washington, who had also been a member of the earlier Mt. Everest Expedition.

CANADA

Senator Kennedy also placed on the snowy cap a copy of his brother's Inaugural Address, the John F. Kennedy Inaugural Medallion, and a few of President Kennedy's P. T.-109 boat tie clasps. The Senator's children, who adored their uncle, pleaded with their father, to bring the tie clasps back. The Senator left one at the summit.

The climbing team also carried an American flag and two Canadian flags to the memorial; one was of the old Union Jack design and the other the newer maple leaf design. Both were imbedded in the sanctified top, symbolizing the unity of the two countries, joined together in memory of the President.

REPUBLIC OF CHINA

While no concrete memorial has been erected to President Kennedy in China, the government, on its own behalf and for the people, contributed the sum of $50,000 to the John F. Kennedy Memorial Library Fund. The presentation was made by the Chinese Nationalist Ambassador Tingfu T. Tsiang, in Washington, D.C., on February 3, 1965, to the late Senator Robert F. Kennedy.

Mrs. Jacqueline Kennedy, on March 17, 1965, expressed her feelings in these words:

> . . . I write to convey my deep thanks to you — and to the people of the Republic of China — for the wonderful gift. . . . It was President Kennedy's treasured hope that a library might be built — one day — and he had so looked forward to planning it himself in the future. Since time denied him this, we must now do it for him — and I can assure you it will be the finest President's library ever.

> The knowledge that the President continues to live in the hearts of so many — throughout the world — touches me deeply, and the fact that your country has chosen this way in which to show their esteem for him means more than I can ever say.

Ciudad Kennedy, Bogota, Colombia

COLOMBIA

President Kennedy's youthful vigor and ardent championship of the Alliance for Progress brought him unparalleled veneration from the people of South America.

His sudden death was a personal blow to each citizen. Sorrow quickly replaced lightheartedness. Crowds wept, dirges and requiems filled the air waves, equaling in many instances and often exceeding the grief which overcame the people of the United States. Within weeks, on December 17, 1963, the government of Colombia issued a multicolored 10-centavos airpost stamp. The stamp told the story of Kennedy and the Alliance for Progress. On the left, facing eastward, was projected the green – and – blue symbol of the Alliance, with the hand holding forth the burning torch; and on the right, the portrait of President Kennedy. The legend on the left contained the Spanish equivalent of the Alliance, Alianza Para El Progreso. Kennedy had himself employed the Spanish when the program was instituted.

On May 16, 1961, President Kennedy said:

COLOMBIA

I am pleased to announce the second project of the
Peace Corps: this time in Colombia. The Colombian
project will train and assign some 64 volunteers in small
farming, handicraft, rural construction, and sanitation.
They will work with already trained Colombian counter-
parts in a joint program sponsored by the private voluntary agency, CARE, and Colombia's Department of
Community Development. There they will assist small
rural communities to develop their own economic resources and educational and sanitary facilities. . . .It is
also gratifying that the Peace Corps is entering a joint
venture with Colombia, with which we have long and
historic ties of friendship. . .

Seven months later, December 17, 1961, the President stood before an
open field and laid the cornerstone for the largest housing project ever built
under the auspices of the Alliance for Progress. Once again, he reiterated his
concern for the welfare of the people, saying, "Alliance for Progress is a
phrase, but I believe that its true significance is here in this field."

The work began feverishly, and some sixteen months later, on April 2,
1963, the President reported to the Congress on the progress of his projects.
In a Special Message, he proudly said:

In Bogota, Colombia, the site of the old airport is be-
coming a new city for seventy-one thousand persons
who are building their own houses. . . .

This year I received a letter from Señor Argemil Plazas
Garcia, whom I met in Bogota upon the dedication of
an Alianza housing project. He writes: 'Today I am living in the house with my thirteen children, and we are
very happy to be free of such poverty and no longer to
be moving around like outcasts. Now we have dignity
and freedom.

My wife and my children and I are writing you this

humble letter, to express to you the warm gratitude of such Colombian friends who now have a home in which they can live happily. . . .'

On the very day the President was assassinated, the decision was made to name the project after him. It is now Ciudad Kennedy (City of Kennedy).

COLOMBIA

The City of Kennedy, or Kennedy City, is an Alliance for Progress town. It is the project which rose where Kennedy stood. About 110,000 people live in the massive project which contains twelve thousand units, and the entire city fronts the blue-brown Andes in the distance. Schools, markets, and homes show the signs of happy use by happier people in a land where hope was dim.

John F. Kennedy will be long remembered in Colombia where so many of its citizens paid for the recital of masses for the repose of his soul, so that the masses will be said for many years to come.

DENMARK

In the Kingdom of Denmark, picture-book land of small green farms, blue lakes, and white beaches, the small country which has taught the world so many lessons — freedom, education, and social legislation — one of the most touching of events took place after the assassination of the late President. In Syvsten, a village of a few hundred, in the northernmost province of Jutland, a lively discussion took place in the parish council on whether one of the roads should be named after John F. Kennedy. Those in favor won the argument by saying: "Even if we are only a tiny dot on the map, President Kennedy nevertheless meant a great deal to us, too."

The fiftieth anniversary of the birth of the late President, May 29, 1967, was marked by the inauguration of the Kennedy Institute for treatment of Folling's disease (phenylketonuria), built in conjunction with the State Hospital in Glostrup, outside Copenhagen.

In memory of the late President, a school in Soborg was named John F. Kennedy Skolen. In Copenhagen, Kennedy Garden, a recreational center comprising day-care centers for infants and school children, youth and parents' clubs, and a club for retired people was established on November 25, 1966. It is the largest center of its kind in Denmark.

In addition, the Danish Government contributed a gift of Danish-designed and manufactured furniture to the John F. Kennedy Center for the Performing Arts in Washington, D.C.

Kennedy Garden, Copenhagen, Denmark

DOMINICAN REPUBLIC

In the West Indies, some six hundred miles southeast of Miami, Florida, lies the island of Hispaniola, discovered by Christopher Columbus in 1492.

Almost five hundred years later, President Kennedy, in his annual message to the Congress, said of this republic, which with Haiti on its western frontier makes up the island, "The people of the Dominican Republic, with our firm encouragement and help, and those of our sister Republics of this Hemisphere are safely passing through the treacherous course from dictatorship through disorder towards democracy. . ."*

On March 13, 1964, the third anniversary of the inception of President Kennedy's Alliance for Progress, was marked by the opening of a primary school in the small town of Las Charcas, ten miles from the capital Santo Domingo. Columbus is buried in Ciudad Trujillo in the Cathedral of Santo Domingo.

The school is named Escuela John F. Kennedy.

* January 11, 1962

FRANCE

When President Kennedy visited Paris in May, 1961, he quoted Benjamin Franklin, first Ambassador of the United States to France, as saying: "Every man has two countries: France and his own." Both the President and his First Lady loved France as a second country.

At his death, a stunned President Charles de Gaulle proclaimed:

"President Kennedy died like a soldier, under fire, in the line of duty, and in the service of his country."

To millions of Frenchmen, the military tribute was too impersonal a tribute to the vigorous American President they had taken to their hearts.

Streets throughout France suddenly witnessed changes, especially towns like Montigny-les Metz and Chateauroux. In France, the name of a street in memory is a tribute limited only to the select few.

Paris joined the ranks. The name of John F. Kennedy became a fifth presidential American name in the streets of Paris. Rue Washington, Rue Lincoln, Rue Wilson, and Avenue Franklin D. Roosevelt had been previously memorialized. These areas string along the Seine River and are associated

Avenue du Président Kennedy

with other immortal names: Rue Franklin, Boulevard Pershing, Rue Christopher Columbus, Rue Edgar Allan Poe, and others.

On March 16, 1964, barely four months after the assassination, Paris paid tribute. In a solemn ceremony, attended by the President's mother, Mrs. Joseph P. Kennedy, the Quai de Passy was renamed Avenue du President Kennedy. It is the longest of the five avenues named for American Presidents. The sign on the wall noted Quai de Passy with a diagonal line crossing through and beneath, in large square letters, the new name of the street.

The naming of the street was initiated in a matter of hours after the President's death. The municipal authorities decided to perpetuate his memory on a main street. The United States Ambassador was contacted and asked to inquire of Mrs. Kennedy how she would prefer the street to be renamed. She replied that her preference would be Avenue rather than the term Quai.

The Avenue du President Kennedy fronts the right bank of the Seine in a fashionable residential area. One block away, under the shadow of famed Eiffel Tower across the street, stands the Palais de Chaillot, where the President on his visit in June, 1961, introduced himself: "I am the man who accompanied Jacqueline Kennedy to Paris and I have enjoyed it."

The official dedication was performed by the President of the City Council, Jean Aubertin. He reflected the feeling of all Frenchmen when he said: "Never, perhaps, has the death of a foreign chief of state so profoundly moved every Frenchman and every Parisian."

GREAT BRITAIN

President Kennedy knew England better than any other foreign country. He had spent a number of summer vacations there as a young man while at college. He had served as his father's special representative when Joseph P. Kennedy was Ambassador to the Court of St. James. President Kennedy's first book, written when he was 29, dealt with England; it was called *Why England Slept*, and analyzed the beginnings of World War II.

As President, Kennedy visited England twice, on June 4, 1961, and exactly two years later, on June 4, 1963.

Upon his sudden death, the people of England began immediately to lay plans for memorials. Said **Sir** Patrick Dean in the United Nations session of homage, November 26, 1963:

> . . .all of us, in all walks of life, recognized that here was a man who, in these years of swift and difficult change, and, on occasion, of sudden and fearful **danger,** had, in the fullest measure, a sureness of vision and a steadfastness of purpose, and we recognized in him that fundamental attachment to ideals which were, and are, ours too. . . .

In the shadow of Coventry, England's new Cathedral, a John F. Kennedy Youth Residence was officially dedicated on April 24, 1964. Its official name, simple and dramatic — The Kennedy House.

British Memorial, Runnymede, Surrey, England

British Memorial, Runnymede, Surrey, England

West Berlin's Mayor Willy Brandt dedicated the residence, saying that the life and actions of the late President had given young people all over the world a new and dynamic sense of purpose.

The West German Ambassador, Herbert Blankenhorn, participated in the ceremonies and presented a gift of $4,200 from the Bonn Government toward the furnishings of The Kennedy House. The Bonn Government and the Berlin City Government together contributed the sum of $14,000 for this purpose.

GREAT BRITAIN

One of the more unusual testimonials to President Kennedy's memory was the educational theme emphasized in Luton, England, a small town thirty miles from London. The Stopsley Secondary Modern School, which has a student enrollment of 1,000, devoted an entire day to the study of the late President and his country, naming it, "John F. Kennedy — Family, Nation, World."

The headmaster explained that the death of President Kennedy had come as a great shock to the teachers and the student body, and ". . .We even wanted to know why and how it could happen. Our hope was greater understanding, even more than greater knowledge. We also wanted to remove the grand illusion that everyone in America drives Cadillacs, lives in penthouses. . ."

The faculty consisted of American residents in Britain, staff members of the American embassy, students of the Fulbright exchange program, captains of industry, journalists of the *New York Times*, and a few Britons who had lived in United States. They took over the classes and sought to describe the policies of President Kennedy and the America in which he lived. They answered such questions from students as, "How can you describe yourselves as a democracy when you deny Negroes the right to vote? Why are all policemen in America Irish?"

Bulletin boards were used to display the theme of the day. Prominent topics were: Negroes in America; the Campaign against Poverty; John F. Kennedy — The Family Man; and The Senseless Tragedy.

Asked what he had learned on that day of study, one twelve-year-old summed it up by saying, "Now I understand why President Kennedy wanted to abolish slavery."

On the first anniversary, November, 1964, following a special mass at Westminster Cathedral, the Royal Philharmonic Orchestra performed the world premiere of *Epilogue to Profiles in Courage*, by the American composer Roy Harris.

The most elaborate and colorful memorial in England is the site near Runnymede Island, dedicated by Her Majesty the Queen of England, on May 14, 1965.

In May, 1964, the Lord Mayor of London had launched a million-dollar President Kennedy National Memorial Appeal. The aims were two-fold: to provide funds for scholarships for British students to attend Harvard University, Massachusetts Institute of Technology, and Radcliffe College, and to erect an appropriate memorial at Runnymede.

The site lies on three acres of meadowland overlooking Runnymede Island, where the Magna Charta was signed by King John in 1215. The selected area had been developed by building a winding footpath through the woodland and up steps, the path and steps being of granite set to last for centuries. At the top of the steps there was erected a large Portland stone weighing seven tons, on which is carved the inscription:

> This acre of English ground was given to the United States of America by the people of Britain in memory of
>
> JOHN F. KENNEDY
>
> President of the United States 1961-1963
> Died by an assassin's hand 22 November 1963
>
> Let every nation know whether it wishes us well or ill that we shall pay any price, bear any burden, meet any hardship, support any friend or oppose any foe in order to assure the survival and success of liberty.
>
> From the inaugural address of
> President Kennedy
> 20th January, 1961

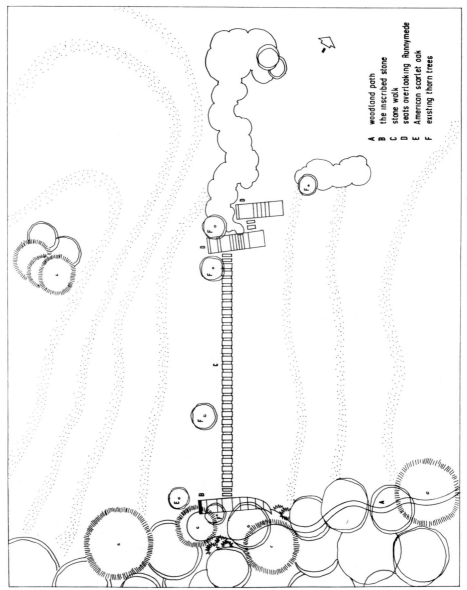

A woodland path
B the inscribed stone
C stone walk
D seats overlooking Runnymede
E American scarlet oak
F existing thorn trees

British Memorial, Runnymede, Surrey, England

British Memorial, Runnymede, Surrey, England

At right angles to the steps, another path, perfectly level, runs into a field and terminates in two stone bench seats, presenting a delightful view of the Thames Valley.

The memorial is the design of G. A. Jellicoe, a member of the Royal Fine Arts Commission, and was dedicated by the Queen on the 750th anniversary of the signing of the Magna Charta, in the presence of Mrs. Jacqueline Kennedy and John F. Kennedy, Jr.

GREAT BRITAIN   The Queen said in her address:

> His readiness to shoulder the burden and the passionate enthusiasm which he brought to his labors . . . gave courage, inspiration and above all new hope not only to Americans but to all America's friends.

> Nowhere was this more true than here in these Islands. With all their hearts, my people shared his triumphs, grieved at his reverses, and wept at his death.

Mrs. Kennedy delivered a statement of thanks:

> My husband loved history . . . and what you have done today in his honor would please him more than my words can express. He had the greatest affection for the British people for what you have accomplished down through the ages in this land, and for what you represent around the world.

> Your literature and the lives of your great men shaped him as did no other part of his education. In a sense he returns today to the tradition from which he sprang.

> To the British people and the John F. Kennedy Memorial Trust I express the deepest gratitude of the people of the United States. For my part, I thank you for inviting me to be here today with my children. One day they will realize what it means to have their father honored at Runnymede.

To all of you who created this memorial I can only say
it is the deepest comfort to me to know that you share
with me thoughts that lie too deep for tears."

The Kennedy Scholarship program began on September 6, 1966, with the arrival of ten scholars, seven to study at Harvard University and three at Massachusetts Institute of Technology, their subjects ranging from land and international relations to mechanical engineering and econometrics. The group was selected from a large field of applicants from universities and colleges of advanced technology in Britain.

These universities were designated because Boston was President Kennedy's home, Harvard his college, and at Cambridge, Massachusetts, the Kennedy family will establish the John F. Kennedy Memorial Library.

The trustees of the Kennedy Memorial Fund have announced that under the Trust, scholarships will be awarded to enable up to twelve Kennedy scholars to spend the academic year 1968 — 1969 at Harvard University (which includes Radcliffe College) or at the Massachusetts Institute of Technology.

On May 15, 1965, the late Senator Robert F. Kennedy unveiled a new bust of his brother at the International Students House on Park Crescent. Commissioned by the Sunday *Telegraph* after an unusual public appeal two days after the assassination, the bronze bust, dominating a small garden in the crescent-shaped back courtyard of the center, was executed by the famed sculptor Jacques Lipchitz.

The inscription tells us that Britons "admired this President for his will of steel and his tongue of silver."

British Memorial, Runnymede, Surrey, England

GREECE

The Prime Minister of Greece visited President Kennedy at the White House on April 17, 1961. The President, welcoming the guest said, among other things:

> Someone once said everyone is either an Athenian or a Spartan — in any case, we are all Greeks in the great sense of recognizing the wellspring from which all our efforts began.
>
> I am sure that sometimes the Greeks get tired of hearing about ancient history, because they are concerned with making history today. But we look to Greece for inspiration, and we look to modern Greece for comradeship. . .

The people of modern Greece, seeking to reciprocate the expression of comradeship, responded to the news of the President's death with a large number of street memorials. Numerous places and avenues memorialized President Kennedy, including the cities of Athens, Salonika, Drama, Kaisariani, Halandri and the island of Rhodes.

HONG KONG

The John F. Kennedy Spastic Childrens Center in Sandy Bay, Hong Kong, was opened officially by Sir David Trench, Governor of Hong Kong, on March 2, 1967.

The Center, gift from the American people through the World Rehabilitation Fund, caters to a maximum of 80 pupils: 60 residential and 20 day pupils of both sexes between the ages of four and fourteen. In addition to providing a suitable general education, the Center offers medical care and therapy.

The cornerstone-laying ceremonies were held on November 26, 1965, led by Congressman Otto E. Passman of Louisiana. Present were Lady Hogan; Lady Trench of the British Red Cross; Mr. Abba Schwartz of the Department of State; Consul General Edward E. Rice, representing the Secretary of State; the Honorable Dhun Ruttonjee; Professor A. R. Hodgson; and Dr. Harry S. Y. Fang.

Congressman Passman said:

> I am very proud that this contribution from the American people to the welfare of handicapped Chinese children in Hong Kong bears the name of our late President

John F. Kennedy. All of us are aware of President Kennedy's concern for and interest in assisting handicapped children. We remember President Kennedy as a great humanitarian, a man of personal warmth for suffering people in all parts of the world. I feel, therefore, that it is fitting that President Kennedy, who was not only the leader of his own people, but an inspiration to the world, should be commemorated here in Hong Kong, by an institution dedicated to helping afflicted children to achieve their greatest potential.

It is with a sense of pride that I lay this cornerstone to the memory of John F. Kennedy and in dedication to a fuller and happier life for those whom this institution will serve.

John F. Kennedy Centre, Sandy Bay, Hong Kong

IRAN

On September 6, 1962, President Kennedy, in a message to the Shah of Iran encouraged:

> . . . Iran has suffered adversity many times before in its 2,500 years of recorded history. But it has always triumphed. . ."

Iran, formerly known as Persia has joined the western world in memorializing President Kennedy.

Less than two months after President Kennedy's death, and in the presence of the late President's brother-in-law, Sargent Shriver, Premier Assadullah Alam dedicated an avenue in the capital city, Teheran, known as Avenue John Fitzgerald Kennedy.

IRELAND

Speaking before the Congress of the United States on May 28, 1964, President Eamon de Valera, describing the warm welcome given to President Kennedy when he visited Ireland in June, 1963, said that Ireland opened its arms "Not merely because of his Irish blood, not merely because of his personal charm nor the qualities of his heart and mind. We honored him because he was regarded by our people as the symbol of this great nation."

The President himself had always regarded Ireland as the symbol of the immigrant and refugee, so important to the development of America. He emphasized this theme in his book *A Nation of Immigrants*. Especially close to his heart was the citizenry of Ireland who had contributed so much to America.

When he arrived in Dublin on his visit to the home of his forebears, he said:

No country in the world, in the history of the world,

has endured the hemorrhage which this island endured over a period of a few years for so many of her sons and daughters. These sons and daughters are scattered throughout the world, and they give this small island a family of millions upon millions who are scattered all over the globe, who have been among the best and most loyal citizens of the countries that they have gone to, but have also kept a special place in their memories, in many cases their ancestral memory, of this green and misty island. So, in a sense, all of them who visit Ireland come home. . . .

The land of President Kennedy's ancestors will again see the name Kennedy written large. Ireland had planned a President Kennedy Memorial Park. The site chosen is at Sliabh Coillte, County Wexford, and the deeds of a 400-acre estate have been handed over to the Minister for Lands. Situated on a commanding hill overlooking the River Barrow, the site is about six miles from Dunganstown, ancestral home of the late President's family.

Dedication ceremonies were held on May 29, 1968. Mrs. Sargent Shriver, sister of the late President and Mrs. Edward Kennedy participated.

The memorial project originated at a meeting of the Irish Institute in December, 1963, when various Irish-American groups undertook to raise the sum of $100,000 towards its realization.

The hill probably derives its name, Mountain of Woods, from the fact that it was densely wooded in ancient times.

The area has been developed into a monument of educational and scientific significance, providing recreational facilities also. It includes an arboretum and forest garden. A residential horticultural school is contemplated within the scope of the project, and it is hoped ultimately to assemble over a thousand specimens of woody plants, of arboricultural, horticultural, and botanical interest. The Forest Garden will also include some three thousand plots of different coniferous and broad-leaved trees, assembled into a plantation.

Twenty two countries with which Ireland has diplomatic relations are

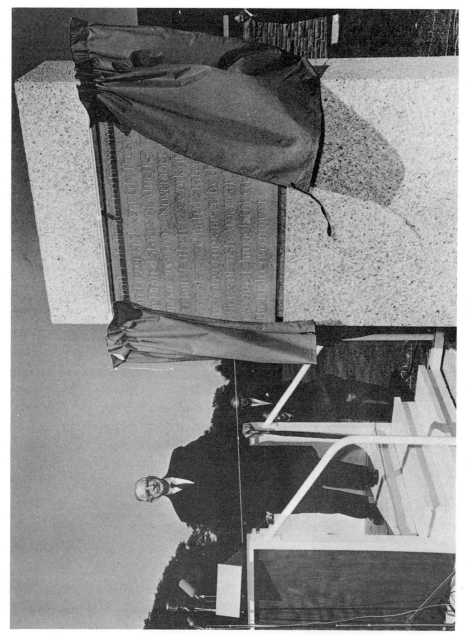

President Kennedy Memorial Park, Sliabh Coillte, County Wexford, Ireland

to send plant contributions for the John F. Kennedy Park and a number of arboreta and similar institutions in many parts of the world have also offered plants.

The twenty two countries are: Argentina, Australia, Austria, Belgium, Canada, Denmark, Finland, France, Germany, Great Britain, India, Italy, Japan, Luxembourg, Netherlands, New Zealand, Portugal, Spain, Sweden, Switzerland, Turkey and the United States.

IRELAND

Ireland is also planning to name a concert hall in Dublin after President Kennedy, which will serve as a cultural center for the entire country.

On the occasion when President de Valera and his wife, Prime Minister Mr. Sean F. Lemass, T. D., and members of the government attended the Solemn Requiem Mass in St. Andrew's Church on the anniversary of President Kennedy's death, a group of twenty-one children flew to the United States to appear on a televised tribute to their hero. The children comprised the choir that sang for President Kennedy when he visited Ireland and he had responded with warmth and gratitude to their performances.

Mrs. Jacqueline Kennedy wrote the following message to President De Valera:

> I do want to thank you Mr. President and thank the Government and people of Ireland and so many descendants of Ireland here in America for making possible these moving ceremonies which will take place there today. I know the care and effort which you have devoted to the John F. Kennedy Park. It will be a memorial that will forever touch our hearts, alive as he will always be for us there in his beloved Ireland.
>
> He was Irish and of nothing was he more proud — the people who were with him at the beginning and those who were with him at the end were Irish. Among his happiest days were those he spent as your guest on his state visit in 1963. Now you honor him in this forest garden, in this green and misty island, to use his words,

which he honored for its devotion to human liberty. He used to read us Yeats:

> Do our woods and winds, and ponds cover
> more quiet woods, more shining winds, more
> star-glimmering ponds: is Eden out of time
> and space?

I am so deeply grateful, Mr. President, that you have chosen to make this Eden for him there. Thank you.

The late President's parents sent the following message:
From President Kennedy's early boyhood years in our Irish neighborhood in Boston to that day in late November when the Irish guard paid final respects at his graveside there was nothing more meaningful and important to him than his Irish heritage. One of the happiest and most memorable events in our son's life was his visit to Ireland in 1963.

He was visibly moved by the warm welcome which he received from the citizens of County Wexford, the home of his forefathers. Our family shall always remember the wonderful hospitality and friendship which you extended to Jack and so we thank you all for the John Fitzgerald Kennedy Memorial Park which looks down on the Kennedy ancestral home in Dunganstown and which will remind people from all over the world of President Kennedy's love for Ireland.

Memorial Building, The John F. Kennedy Peace Forest, Hills of Jerusalem, Israel

ISRAEL

Long before he became President of the United States, John F. Kennedy's interest in Israel was keen and unequivocal.

On November 27, 1956, speaking before the Histadrut Organization in Baltimore, Maryland, he said:

> . . .the character of the Middle East will be shaped for generations to come by one factor which was not present a generation ago — the State of Israel. It is time that all the nations of the world, in the Middle East and elsewhere, realized that Israel is here to stay. . . .

Two years later, on the floor of the Senate, and commenting on the Tenth Anniversary of the establishment of Israel, he said:

> . . .the history of Israel reaches back 3,000 years, yet Israel is one of the new nations of the world. I think the re-creation of Israel, after a long period when its citizens were in exile throughout the world, is easily one of the most dramatic stories in history. The courage and devotion with which its citizens have defended their in-

dependence during the past decade is heartening to the friends of freedom everywhere. The strong friendship which has existed between Israel and the United States since the days of Israel's rebirth has served as a source of support to us in our efforts to protect the interests of the free world everywhere.

ISRAEL   Innumerable memorials have been erected and planned in Israel.

The world-famed Hadassah Hospital in Jerusalem, adjacent to the chapel which houses the twelve magnificent Chagall windows, is the background for the new John F. Kennedy Information Center, erected with contributions from American Hadassah members. Hadassah is the Women's Zionist Organization. Dedication ceremonies were held on November 10, 1966, in the presence of United States Ambassador Walworth Barbour; Teddy Kollek, Mayor of Jerusalem; and 150 Hadassah representatives led by Mrs. Mortimer Jacobson, President.

Designed to reflect the late President's concern for underprivileged youth, the Women's American Ort, in cooperative sponsorship with the Jerusalem municipality, has established a new 2,000-student apprentice training center in Bocca, the northern section of Israel.

The Weizmann Institute of Science in Rehovot, Israel, has established a series of 46 John F. Kennedy Research Awards, one for each year the late President lived. The scholarships and fellowships are awarded to scholars selected by an internationally renowned committee. They will come from the Institute's John F. Kennedy Memorial Foundation, which will eventually amount to one million Israeli pounds.

On the grounds of the Institute, named after Chaim Weizmann, first President of Israel, a permanent memorial has been created. It is the Weizmann Menorah or The Burning Bush Menorah, the work of the distinguished New York-born Beverly Pepper, who lives and works in Rome, Italy. The theme of the Menorah is a memorial to President Kennedy. It represents the dual Shaddai (Almighty) and the Blessing, the epitome of the Burning Bush. Twenty-eight feet high, the Menorah weighs four tons and is made of Terminose stainless steel and rests on a 16-ton base of Tiberius basalt granite.

Memorial Building, The John F. Kennedy Peace Forest, Hills of Jerusalem, Israel

Burning Bush Menorah, Rehovot, Israel

On the hallowed ground where Bar Kochba waged his gallant battle for Judea's freedom (131-135 C.E.), the John F. Kennedy Peace Forest has risen, planted by Jews of America through the Jewish National Fund, and dedicated to the everlasting peace and bonds of friendship that link the United States and the State of Israel.

The Kennedy Forest will comprise millions of trees, each to be a living, verdant symbol of the freshness of vision and the inspiration the late President brought to the White House.

At the entrance to this noble forest, an unusual edifice has risen into the sky. High on the hills of Judea, overlooking Jerusalem, a massive structure of fifty concrete columns in a circular enclosure, each column representing a state of the union, towers on the landscape. It is simple in design, yet offers the feeling of strength and dignity and moving power. The two-story round structure, seven and one half meters high and almost seventy meters in circumference, commands the terrain. Its gray white lines rise in the shape of a broad-stemmed, upsweeping tree trunk, and then cut — like the tragically severed life of President Kennedy. Inside the memorial, one also gets the feeling of space and fullness. A single shaft of light streams down from the round opening in the specially formed sawtooth ceiling. Except for the sculptured bust of President Kennedy, the memorial is empty. A Book of Remembrance stands waiting for visitors to write their names.

Each of fifty pylons will have the emblem of the state it represents, and narrow glass walls between the columns offer a magnificent view of the young forests and ageless rock across the hills as far as the eye can see.

The memorial is the design of famed Israeli architect David Reznik.

Speaking at the event which formally declared the establishment of this Peace Forest, the late Senator Robert F. Kennedy said:

> The spirit that my brother and I witnessed in Israel was the kind of spirit that made the United States the great nation that it is — that's why President Kennedy felt so close to Israel. . . .
>
> I bring you the appreciation of Mrs. John F. Kennedy and the rest of the Kennedy family for what you are

doing here tonight. . ... I was in Israel in 1948, in 1949, and again in 1951, and the growth in those few short years was so great, it amazed me. We in the Kennedy family are deeply appreciative to you for establishing the John F. Kennedy Peace Forest in Israel."*

ISRAEL

Dedication ceremonies were conducted on July 4, 1967. The Hon. Earl Warren, Chief Justice of the United States Supreme Court, delivered the dedication address.

The Bar Ilan University of Israel has established a John F. Kennedy Chair in American Civilization, which has as its announced purpose the hope to "increase Israel's understanding of the ingredients of American social and political institutions."

The occupants of the chair will consist of distinguished American educators, academicians, and students of the arts and culture of all faiths and creeds.

*November 29, 1964, Beverly Hilton Hotel, Beverly Hills, California.

ITALY

A massive 18-by-6 foot granite block sculpture, rising on a grassy knoll in the Piazzale delle Canestre in Rome's beautiful Borghese Gardens, memorializes John F. Kennedy in the Eternal City. The block of wall was created by Amerigo Tot and chosen by *Vita* magazine after a closed competition in which many leading artists submitted designs. In bold relief, the memorial portrays in stone a broken spear, resembling a nail about to penetrate the concrete wall. The pear shaft, of polished bronze, and the end, smashed flat, reveal a sculptured profile of the late President, three feet in diameter. Four smaller nails, projecting from the shaft, form a cross.

Amerigo Tot, known best in Rome for his friezes in the Stazione Termini, a 66-foot ceramic in the Palazzo dello Sport, and winner of the Grand Prix de Rome (1933-1936), described his creation:

> The nail is the symbol of martyrs, and we are living today under psychological pressures in which walls are everywhere; walls between society and society, nation and nation, and person and person.
>
> Kennedy was surrounded by a thousand walls — of race, nationality, inequality, everything — all the stupid rivalries that there are, and he tried to break them down but he never quite succeeded, because he was killed.

The third anniversary of President Kennedy's death was the date of official dedication of the monument.

Italy's second largest city, Milan, on August 29, 1964, dedicated the Centro Sportive Comunale Presidente Kennedy, the President Kennedy Sport Center. In colorful ceremonies, the United States Ambassador to Rome, G. Frederick Reinhardt, accepted the memorial on behalf of his country.

ITALY The Sport Center, largest of its kind in Italy, contains a number of athletic fields for all sports — baseball, soccer, tennis, and facilities for other Olympic tournaments. It is fronted by a series of specially constructed beautiful gardens and will become the center of athletic competitions for Europe.

On March 19, 1967, earth from the grave of President Kennedy and from St. Patrick's hill in Ireland were mixed in an urn and placed in the cornerstone of a church to be erected near Parma, Italy, to the memory of the late President and dedicated to St. Patrick. Patrick Kennedy, a relative of the President, bore the earth from Ireland, and Earl T. Crain, United States Consul in Milan brought the earth from the Kennedy grave.

Bishop Evasio Colli of Parma blessed the cornerstone at the close of the ceremonies.

Memorial, Borghese Gardens, Rome, Italy

Centro Sportive Comunale, Milan, Italy

KENYA

Kenya, in East Africa, was named after the highest mountain within its borders, Mount Kenya. A number of establishments have been named for President Kennedy, all of them educational institutions.

There are three President Kennedy high schools in Nairobi, Kitale, and Nakuru. Egerton College in Njoro dedicated a dining room to the President's memory. A secondary school at Mombasa is called Kennedy and the New Era College in Nairobi named its library for John F. Kennedy.

The library was dedicated on November 25, 1965, by John Hogan, head of the United States Information Service in Nairobi. Speaking at the ribbon-cutting ceremonies, he said: "It is fitting that another educational institution should perpetuate his memory in this way. President Kennedy dedicated himself to youth and education."

The principal of the college, Mr. V. P. Sharma, stated that the idea for the establishment of the library came from his own son, K. B. Sharma, vice-principal, who had traveled extensively in the United States and Canada. While visiting the grave in Washington, he conceived the idea of perpetuating the name of the fallen President with the establishment of a library at the college. The library will contain a permanent collection of books written by and about John F. Kennedy.

NEW ZEALAND

The first country in the world to allow women to vote, the first to provide old-age pensions for all, the first to compel management and labor to submit their disputes to arbitration, has, with the consent of Mrs. Jacqueline Kennedy, established a John Fitzgerald Kennedy Memorial Fund, — the initial target set for $150,000.

The purpose of the fund is to enable Americans eminent in academic life, literature, or public affairs to visit the land that lies some 1,200 miles southeast of Australia, to lecture and meet a wide cross-section of New Zealanders.

The Prime Minister of New Zealand, the Rt. Hon. K. J. Holyoake, in announcing the fund in Wellington, the country's capital, said:

> The people we have in mind for fellowships under the Kennedy Fund would be of the highest standing in their own fields and therefore best able to illuminate the ideals and purpose to which the late President devoted his life. The Government would like to think of this Fund and the work it would do as keeping President Kennedy's memory green in the minds of New Zealanders.

We see the Fund as reaffirming this country's commitment to the aims of peace and social justice which President Kennedy pursued with such clear-sightedness, generosity and vigor and which his tragic and untimely death prevented him from carrying to fulfillment.

NEW ZEALAND

There is already ample provision made for the exchange between the United States and New Zealand, of students, teachers and research scholars, as well as opportunity for New Zealanders outstanding in politics, journalism and other fields of public activity to travel to the United States. The Kennedy Fund, although necessarily limited in its scope, would enable us to bring leading Americans to this country to give us the benefit of their experience and their insights; at the same time it would allow them to learn more about New Zealand and its attitudes.

PERU

On December 23, 1963, just a month after the assassination of President Kennedy, the first of many ceremonies destined to take place throughout the world was held in Peru, land of the Incas, third largest country of South America. In Miraflores, the President of the Republic, in the presence of United States Ambassador Wesley Jones; the Mayor of Miraflores, Alfonso Benes; famed architect Fernando Selaunde Terry; Cabinet members and diplomatic representatives, dedicated the John F. Kennedy Park. Thus Miraflores became the first city in the world to pay public tribute to President Kennedy.

The John F. Kennedy Park is located at the crossroads of four streets — Lima, Miraculous Virgin, Marshal Benavides, and Schell. It covers an area of 8,200 square meters.

In the midst of the park, almost at its center, stands a majestically executed bronze bust of the President, the work of sculptor Alfredo Orosio. The bust is based on a composition representing the head of the President gazing into the distance, placed on a pedestal of black marble which emerges from a mirror of water.

The following legend appears on one of the sides of the pedestal, a quotation from President Kennedy:

> In the future there shall exist a hemisphere where all
> men will have food and an opportunity to work.

John F. Kennedy

Beneath this quotation the President's signature is graven in bronze.

John Fitzgerald Kennedy Park, Miraflores, Peru

SOUTH KOREA

An era, clearing darkness, should have dawned,
When you, like a morning star,
Scintillated in glory. . .but now,
Nightly mist still lingers
About this gate of peace you built.
Your name, we so miss, J. F. Kennedy:
This friend of great ideas and intelligence.

You flame eternally at Arlington,
You will be endeared in every good heart.
We always remember you astride
The wall of hatred you crushed agape
Your name, we so miss, J. F. Kennedy:
This friend of courage, and vitality.

These words were written by Koo Sang, the president of the Korean Poets Society, who with many distinguished citizens of Korea, including the President of the Republic, the President of the Han Yang University, and the former United Nations Ambassador, responded to the dynamic efforts of a young artist, Song Doo-Young, to create a Kennedy Memorial Cultural Center in Tonguchon, Korea.

Kennedy Memorial Cultural Center, Tonguchon, South Korea

The thirty six year old Doo-Young tells of his emotions when news of the assassination flashed through the Land of the Morning Calm.

> All my respect, admiration and spiritual reliance on John F. Kennedy for his great virtue of spiritual grace and decency seemed to have ended. But the next moment an inspiration flashed through me and directed me to face a canvas and to depict the very John F. Kennedy who had lived within me and thus keep his image as alive as it had always been.

SOUTH KOREA

The portrait was painted and presented to the late Robert F. Kennedy by the artist.

Mrs. Jacqueline Kennedy, upon receipt of the portrait, expressed her appreciation of the cordial friendship from Korea.

Mr. Song Doo Young, however, sought to perpetuate the memory of President Kennedy. He organized the J. F. Kennedy Memorial Society of Korea and laid plans for the creation of an appropriate memorial in Tongu-chon, a city of some 50,000, thirty miles north of Seoul.

Ground was broken on November 26, 1964.

The Cultural Center houses a library, theater, art exhibition hall, and a large community meeting room.

SWITZERLAND

Near Bern, Switzerland, a memorial stone on the hill of "Chutzen" was dedicated on October 23, 1964, by a private organization known as "Pro Liberata." The stone is hewn out of alpine granite and is about 4 1/2 feet high.

In Memoriam

Memorial Photograph Page, *USSR-Soviet Life Today*

UNION OF SOVIET SOCIALIST REPUBLICS

Russian leaders, academicians, poets, artists, and groups of all kinds poured heartfelt words of sympathy to President Johnson, Secretary of State Dean Rusk, and the Kennedy Family, when news of the assassination was flashed throughout the Soviet Union.

The *USSR, Soviet Life Today,* illustrated monthly published in Washington, quickly printed a special four-page supplement to its December 1963 issue. The cover portrayed the official picture of the President, black-bordered, with the words "In Memoriam" in Old English type. Three full pages followed, with expressions of condolence. From Chairman N. Khrushchev and Soviet leaders Anastas I. Mikoyan and Foreign Minister Andre Gromyko, from Nina Krushcheva, Dmitri Shostakovich, from famed ballerina Maya Plisetskaya, poet Sergei Mikhalkov. . .came the words of profound loss.

Nikita Khrushchev recalled from the Kremlin:

> I shall remember President Kennedy as a person of broad outlook who realistically assessed a situation and tried to find ways for negotiated settlements of the international problems which now divide the world.

A large group of Soviet leaders, officers of the Institute of Soviet-American relations, wired President Johnson:

> The Soviet people, together with the American people, share the feeling of profound loss in connection with the tragic death of John Fitzgerald Kennedy, outstanding statesman, U. S. President.

UNION OF SOVIET SOCIALIST REPUBLICS

> While President, John Kennedy strove to improve the international atmosphere.
>
> John Kennedy's understanding and profound interest in all countries, in a just and permanent peace, and in ending the arms race, found a great response among the Soviet public.
>
> Being a realistic-minded politician, he saw that the normalization of relations between our countries is in accord with the vital interests of both peoples and facilitates the strengthening of world peace. Accept our sincere condolences.

Signatories to the telegram included the Rector of the Moscow University, Ivan Petrovsky; Academician Ivan Artobolevsky; film producer Sergei Gerasimov; writer Alexander Korneichuk; *Pravda* commentator Yuri Zhukov; and sociologist Yuri Frantzev.

Valentin Katayev, Soviet writer, expressed his deep sense of loss, saying:

> Kennedy, to my mind, will go down in American history as one of the noblest political leaders, who tried as much as he could to promote the relaxation of international tension and sincerely strove for world peace.
>
> I express my feelings of commiseration. . .with all the Americans whom I happened to meet and become friendly with in the United States: actors, writers, engineers, professors, artists, publishers and diplomats.

I call upon them to fight for the cause of world peace
and, the main thing, to be vigilant.

Academicians Vladimir Veksler, laureate of the 1963 Atoms for Peace Prize and Leonid Sedov, of the Soviet War Veterans Committee, and various press agencies shared their feelings of loss.

The Soviet Women's Committee sent a telegram to the President's widow, expressing the "hope that John F. Kennedy's good deeds, aimed at strengthening mutual understanding and friendship between our peoples, will be continued."

UNION OF SOVIET SOCIALIST REPUBLICS

Alexander Alexandrov, Rector of Leningrad University and Corresponding Member of the USSR Academy of Sciences, represented the depth of loss of many scientists when he said:

> With a group of scientists of Leningrad University I visited Harvard University, of which John F. Kennedy was a graduate. The U. S. President had done a great deal to normalize relations between the USSR and the USA. I can give as an example our own university, where young American scientists are systematically getting acquainted with our achievements, while our scientists are studying at U. S. universities. The lecturers and students of Leningrad University are grieved over John F. Kennedy's death. We express our deep condolences to the family of the deceased, to the lecturers of Harvard University, and to the American people.

John F. Kennedy Memorial Tablet, Town Hall, Berlin-Schoeneberg

WEST GERMANY

In June, 1963, John F. Kennedy visited West Berlin, saw the dread wall, symbol of the ugly imprisonment of humanity, and proclaimed:

> Two thousand years ago the proudest boast was '*civis Romanus sum*.' Today, in the world of freedom, the proudest boast is '*Ich bin ein Berliner*.'

> . . .All free men, wherever they may live, are citizens of Berlin, and, therefore, as a free man, I take pride in the words, '*Ich bin ein Berliner*.'

A year later, his brother, the late Senator, Robert F. Kennedy, in the presence of 70,000 people, unveiled a bronze memorial plaque on the facade of the West Berlin City Hall, and reaffirmed his brother's words.

> I know what he meant when he surveyed the wall of shame and measured it against your courage and said, '*Ich bin ein Berliner*'. . .

> Surrounded by hostility, besieged by enemies, your future threatened, your freedom in jeopardy, you have emerged from each of these assaults, stronger, greater and more resolute. . .For this President Kennedy congratulated you and on behalf of free men everywhere he thanked you. . . .

The man from Pittsburgh is not free until the man from Peiping is free...The man from West Berlin is not free until his brother from East Berlin is also free....

Here on the front line of freedom you serve not only for yourselves and for your country; you defend freedom for my country. You stand with your allies and you defend freedom for free men everywhere.

Soon thereafter, on December 16, 1964, the German-American Community School was officially named the John F. Kennedy School. It was originally started as a joint German-American experiment to determine whether German and American children could be taught simultaneously in two languages. The experiment was highly successful. It grew into an enrollment of over four hundred children and now carries the name of the hero of all youth.

On January 26, 1967, the John F. Kennedy Institute for American Studies was dedicated at the West Berlin Free Universities. Containing one of the largest libraries of Americana in Europe, the structure was formerly a grammar school and was converted at a cost of $250,000, which was provided by the Ford Foundation.

John F. Kennedy Promenade Park, Offenbach-on-Main, West Germany

John F. Kennedy Memorial Tablet, Town Hall, Berlin-Schoeneberg

Kennedy Bridge, Munich, West Germany

YUGOSLAVIA

In the Balkan land of folk heroes, John F. Kennedy has already become a figure of national lore. Today he is the favorite subject of a folk ballad, symbol of hero worship.

The song was composed by a young Bosnian named Ramo Ramovic, who works by day as a bookkeeper and at night sings the ballad in the basement club of the Europa Hotel. He strums to his own accompaniment on a single-stringed *guisla*, an ancient instrument that produces a haunting whine.

The ballad is in the ten-syllable style of Bosnian folksongs, with verses in rhymed couplets. A free translation follows:

"Assassination of John Kennedy."*

Not even the bird that makes its nest,
Could know the disaster was coming,
That the twentieth century
Would herald sad news to all,
That on November twenty-second
America would be in great sorrow.
Echoes ring and phones buzz.
Tempests and storms appear.
Sad news spreads everywhere,
Of America's severe misfortune.
Grief has stirred the whole world,
Kennedy could not be rescued.
The powder was exploded,
The rifle fired from a high floor

*Reprinted from the *New York Times*, July 12, 1964, by permission.

The steel bullet was swift,
That caused John's lethal wounds.
It struck his heroic head,
He met that bitter glory.
Grave pains overcame him,
John fell in Jacqueline's arms.
That dear Jacqueline embraced him
With her white arms.
With a sick heart she embraced him,
To lighten his heavy pains.
With grave suffering darkening his face
They went to Dallas hospital.
Doctors offered help,
In vain; sad news is spreading,
That cursed steel bullet,
Has wounded Johnny mortally.
President Johnny has passed away,
He has left the earth forever.
The news is heard afar,
The world echoes sorrowing despair,
John Kennedy is no more.
Dallas, Texas, what is happening in thee?
Why did you allow that hostile hand,
That "Sniper" to touch that firearm,
So that iron ignited the fire,
And struck John so cunningly,
Johnny has no more strength,
With a sick heart his breathing slows,
Dead Johnny falls to earth.
And now Jacqueline suffers heavy grief.
A beautiful person, respected lady
Stays alone without Johnny.
She will never forget him,
Johnny was like blooming flowers.

They tried to save him
In unlucky Dallas' hospital.
The first aid given him
Kept him not one hour.
That wound was mortal
And the earth has seized him forever,
To rest for eternity,

YUGOSLAVIA   For there was no cure for Johnny.
Now in sorrow many hearts were silent,
And they drove him to the White House
To give him the last honors,
They knew for certain John was gone.
The caisson carries him,
With a white horse from the White House,
To the soldiers' grave of heroes.
This is, Johnny, your eternal home.
The procession turns aside now,
Men of noble face.
All America grieves for him,
There are many foreign friends,
Many notables from abroad.
There are many from all sides,
The chieftains, czars and queens,
And many eminent guests,
To say farewell to the great hero,
Too many to enumerate.
The relatives go first,
With his wife Jacqueline.
In the line are two brothers now,
The grieving Robert next to brother Edward,
And his daughter Caroline,
Who is only six years old.

HOMAGE ON STAMPS

HOMAGE ON STAMPS

No other personage has ever caused such excitement in the philatelic world. Thirty-four countries memorialized Franklin Delano Roosevelt after his death in 1945. John F. Kennedy's expressive countenance — serious, beaming, smiling — in a variety of designs, portraits, or sketches, profile or front-face, in the most alluring and exquisite colors, is impressed on hundreds of stamps of over sixty countries around the globe. Many fascinating scenes of his life, episodes of childhood, youth, college days, Naval service, and his vigorous role in the world, especially in South and Central American lands, are imaginatively and captivatingly depicted on stamps of many countries, in all denominations.

The color combinations are often striking: black and green (Jordan), brown, blue, and carmine (Nicaragua), deep brown and bright pink (Niger), red-brown, blue-green, and dark brown (Mauritania), rose claret and black (Congo), ocher and black (Dubai), red-lilac and deep olive (Ahman), and blue orange, and black (Yemen Arab Republic), and many others.

The shapes are many besides plain square or rectangle land stamps, Jordan's triangular stamp, Sierra Leone's fourteen issues of the first free-form cutouts in the shape of the map of that country, on self-adhesive paper.

None of the stamps are simple; each is carefully planned and engraved and colored, according to the country's way of expressing admiration and individuality.

Brazil, Cameroon, the Central African Republic, Chad (the pose expresses President Kennedy's forceful speaking manner, his extended arm emphasizing the point, face firm, chin determined); the Congo (Brazzaville); the Congo (Leopoldville-Republique Democratique du Congo): Costa Rica; Dahomey; the Dominican Republic; Dubai; Gabon; West Germany; Ghana; Ivory Coast; Liberia; Maldive Islands; Mali; Mauritania; Monaco; New Guinea; Niger; Panama; Papua; the Philippines; Quatar (overprinted with the name and years of the President); Ras al Khaima; Salvador (the President is seen on the rostrum delivering his Inaugural Address); San Marino; Senegal; Upper Volta; Uruguay. All exhibit the face of John F. Kennedy in various poses and moods.

In addition to the portrait, some countries have suggested barely visible symbols, such as wreaths, flags both American and that of the country of issuance. Guinea shows the American flag at half mast.

Other countries, more elaborately and definitively, have combined prominent symbols, equating the person and the idea expressed by the symbol. Thus, Honduras has overprinted on Lincoln stamps the words, "In Memoriam, John F. Kennedy, 22 Novembre 1963," suggesting the greatness of President Kennedy beside the Great Emancipator. Khor Fakkan has sketched the Statue of Liberty alongside the President as does Sharjah and dependencies. Togo's stamp shows the white beauty of the White House beside the President's face, and also on its Lincoln stamps has imprinted the legend "En memoire de John F. Kennedy, 1917 — 1963." Rwanda depicts the President at a telephone with a communications satellite orbiting the earth. The Yemen Arab Republic's contribution is a space set, with space symbols. Paraguay shows a series of satellites, receding into the distance, suggesting a succession of satellites prepared to project another age. Monaco, which has a satellite plunging skyward, has imprinted — and the only country to do so — the President's words from his Inaugural Address: "Ask not what your country can do for you — ask rather what you can do for your country."

On September 4, 1965, Paraguay issued stamps showing not only the President and scenes from his life but also his association with the Alliance for Progress, symbols of flight into space, and a picture of the President with John Glenn and President Johnson. A souvenir sheet of the last-named episode was also issued on the same day.

ARGENTINA

BRAZIL

CHAD

CHILE

COLOMBIA

DOMINICAN REPUBLIC

GABON

GUATEMALA

IVORY COAST

MALI

MAURITANIA

MONACO

REPUBLIC OF CENTRAL AFRICA

SENEGAL

TOGO

Some countries, as though responding to the President's pledge in his Inaugural Address, "To our sister republics south of the border, we offer a special pledge — to convert our good words into good deeds — in a new alliance for progress — to assist free men and free governments in casting off the chains of poverty," have emphasized his role in their country's progress and development, especially the Alliance for Progress.

Many of the South and Central American countries have issued stamps memorializing the President and celebrating the existence and the anniversaries of the Alliance. Argentina, Bolivia, the Canal Zone, Chile, Colombia, Equador, Honduras, Nicaragua, Peru — along with the United States, have engraved the words Alianza Para El Progreso on their stamps, in English or Spanish. Some countries south of the United States border have commemorated the President's visit to their country, — Guatemala and Mexico. The Bahamas issued a stamp commemorating Kennedy's visit with Prime Minister Macmillan in December, 1962.

There are countries which have resurrected the life and events of John F. Kennedy with photographs showing him as a boy, youth, college student, on the PT boat in the Navy, a young father and husband enjoying excursions with his family, and also his relaxation on the famous rocking chair. These scenes have been recorded on stamps in Ajman, the Yemen Kingdom, Paraguay, Fujeria, and Venezuela. The Mutawakelite Kingdom of Yemen has issued a souvenir sheet of President Kennedy and his family, the Eternal Light shown on one side and the Statue of Liberty on the other, with the national flags flanking the family portrait. A number of countries chose to impress on stamps the tragic scenes of the funeral. Umm Al Qiwain, for example, issued stamps showing the caissons in the procession, the riderless horse, the presidential family in mourning, the world's leaders in sorrowful countenance, and also the graveside services. Ecuador shows the President's son John-John at attention saluting the flag-draped coffin.

Each country's stamp is unique for its color combination, message, and expression of esteem. Some are more distinct than others. Cyprus, for example, imprinted the legend, "Self-determination for Cyprus," from a statement President Kennedy made on March 13, 1956. Nigeria has produced a souvenir sheet which shows Mrs. Kennedy and her children. The legend reads:

"In Memoriam, John Fitzgerald Kennedy, who dedicated his life to the promotion of peace." A souvenir sheet of the Maldive Islands displays a large wreath encompassing four stamps with the words, "Let no man of peace and freedom despair," spoken by the President at the United Nations on September 25, 1961. The map of Sierra Leone is lithographed in four colors bearing the names of her principal cities, terrain, rivers, and railways. The slogan, "Land of Iron and Diamonds," is arched across the top. The ordinary series finds the legend, "Honours John F. Kennedy/ American Patriot/ World Humanitarian/ 1917-1963," and below, a curved line reading, "Friend of the African People." The airmail stamp bears the same wording. South Arabia (Kathiri) in February, 1967, included a 1 1/2 shilling stamp of John F. Kennedy in the "Searchers for Peace" series.

On May 29, 1967, what would have been the President's fiftieth birthday, the United States issued an 11-cent stamp, red-and-blue air-letter sheet, and 500 million five-cent blue-and-gray stamps. The rectangle stamp is divided into two equal portions. One exhibits the President's intent, thoughtful portrait; the other, the Eternal Flame. Around the stamp's rim are the dramatic words from his Inaugural Address, ". . . and the glow from that fire can truly light the world."

UPPER VOLTA

UNITED STATES

YEMEN ARAB REPUBLIC

HOMAGE ON MEDAL AND METAL

HOMAGE ON MEDAL AND METAL

Hundreds of sculptured impressions of John F. Kennedy's likeness have been struck on medals, coins, tokens, and jewel pieces. Many date back to the days of his inauguration, in commemoration of that event. Others record his triumphant visits to countries around the world — in symbol, word, and legend. Many strikings record the sorrow of the American people at his untimely death; still others, from twelve nations, on hundreds of medals of cupro-nickel, bronze, jasper, gold, cameo, some elongated, most of them round, others square or oblong, but all with tenderness reflect their burden of grief.

Like a miniature United Nations, the roll call includes Austria, Canada, China, France, Germany, Italy, Mexico, Netherlands, Sharjah (the Persian Gulf State ruled by Sheik Saque bin Sultan Al Quasini), Switzerland, Taiwan (Formosa), and Venezuela. Germany leads all the rest in number of issues, closely followed by Italy, Canada, and Austria.

The medallions tell touching stories and give evidence of the feelings of the people. They portray the face of the President, mostly gazing to the left, others looking forward, still others three-quarters forward. Some have legends inscribed around the rim of the minted piece; others merely set forth his face

✦The author expresses appreciation to Edward C. Rochette, author of *The Medallic Portraits of John F. Kennedy* (A Descriptive Catalogue of The Coins, Medals, Tokens and Store Cards Struck in His Name), issued by Krause Publications, Iola, Wisconsin, 1966.

in relief. Some picture him in serious pose, others project a smiling countenance. The obverse side usually carries the legend and the purpose.

Many medals record President Kennedy's remarks and utterances, which have already begun to reverberate through history. His famed quotation, delivered at the inauguration ceremonies in Washington, appears on a number of coins, including the Hong Kong, Italian, and Taiwan (Formosa) Memorial Medals. Others, more uniquely created, seek to relay his messages in a special way. The Franco-Tedesca Medal of Italy portrays the United States coat-of-arms with the legend: "A MAN DOES WHAT HE MUST — IN SPITE OF PERSONAL CONSEQUENCES" — and circumscribing the design are the words: "35TH PRESIDENT OF THE UNITED STATES."

On the obverse side of a World Personalities Series minted in Italy stands, sharply centered, the American eagle and Kennedy's succinct assertion: "PEACE AND FREEDOM DO NOT COME CHEAP."

In Germany, Kennedy's dynamic message, delivered at St. Paul's Church, in Frankfort, "FREEDOM IS MORE THAN THE REJECTION OF TYRANNY" appears on a medal struck like a commemorative stamp, square rather than round. In another issue in the same country, known as the Kennedy-Lincoln Medal, both martyred Presidents are interlinked. One side has the faces of both; the other side shows a Negro family — father, mother and child — with outstretched shackled hands holding a laurel branch, and the legend: "YOU CAN STOP MEN, YOU CAN'T STOP THEIR IDEAS."

Another Lincoln-Kennedy theme comes from Mexico, depicting President Kennedy by a three-quarter view with the words "PALADIN DE LOS DERECHOS CIVILES JFK." On the reverse, a symbolic design illustrates the freeing of the slaves. In the center is a full view of Lincoln's head; below are crossed hands holding a kneeling slave on the left and a freed man on the right. In the background above the hands the indicator from the scales of justice and the shackles of a slave below are depicted. An American flag forms a complete backdrop. The date 1965 appears above. The border bears the legend: "LIBERATOR DE LOS ASCLAVOS A. LINCOLN."

"THE RIGHTEOUSNESS OF OUR CAUSE MUST UNDERLIE OUR STRENGTH JFK" was selected for the Righteousness Medal issued in Germany and encased in a wreath capped by a star. A French medal reveals an

AUSTRIA

AUSTRIA

CANADA

CANADA

CANADA

CANADA

FRANCE

HONG KONG

outer circle of stylistic stars with the citation, "LES PROBLEMES SONT CREES PAR L'HOMME ILS PEUVENT DONC ETRE RESOLUS PAR L'HOMME" (The problems that are created by man can be resolved by man. John F. Kennedy.)

The obverse side of a Netherlands medal speaks of Kennedy as "A NOBLE SERVANT OF PEACE," and on the reverse side a man on horseback is portrayed slaying serpents of evil, with the words: "A MAN DOES" at the left and "WHAT HE MUST" at the right.

A great many medals depict the tributes of peoples and nations, some in simple design, others more elaborately conceived.

Germany's Defensor Liberatis Medal has the Statue of Liberty surrounded by a field of fifty stars in the lower background; arching the upper edge are the words: "DEFENSOR LIBERATIS" (Defender of Freedom). A more detailed coin shows the hand of Liberty with a torch, and below the bell, the motto "FRIEDEN IN FREIHEIT" (Peace in Freedom). Around the lower half of the medal the grief is narrated "ZUR ERINNERUNG AN DEN TODESTAG" (In memory of the day he died).

The Mexican Memorial series pays tribute most lavishly, with the story in Spanish, Italian, German, Russian, French, and Hebrew. The engraved narration says, "AN IMMORTAL TOKEN TO THE PRESIDENT OF THE UNITED STATES OF NORTH AMERICA, SACRIFICED IN THE SUMMIT OF HIS CAREER, DEVOTED TO THE ACHIEVEMENT OF THE WORLD DESERVES THE HIGHEST ESTEEM OF ALL THE PEOPLES OF THE EARTH, 1917-1963." Austria's Mint issue declares: ER STARB AUCH FUR UNSERE FREIHEIT" (He died also for our freedom). The feelings of the German people in the inscription of a Bavarian Mint issue are expressed in the words: "WIR ALLE HABEN IHN VERLOREN" (We all share his loss), the date, a wreath and a fallen cross.

One of the first memorials was struck in Canada after being modeled in Ireland, dated December 15, 1963, and sent to the late President's parents. The coin shows a draped American flag over a cross and circumscribed by the legend: "HE DIED FOR THE SAKE OF FREEDOM."

Another striking tribute medal shows a wreath of Canadian maple leaves, the Parliament buildings of Ottawa at the bottom, a rocking chair

ITALY

ITALY

ITALY

MEXICO

above, and within the embracing wreath the inscription: "IN TRIBUTE TO THE MEMORY OF PRESIDENT JOHN FITZGERALD KENNEDY UNITED STATES OF AMERICA. HE HAD VISIONS OF NOBILITY FOR ALL MANKIND THAT TRANSCENDED MAN'S COMMON HERITAGE."

In keeping with this form of tribute there is the Political Leaders of the World series, minted in Germany, portraying a globe with the flags of the world. The legend on the outer side, in many languages, reads: "POLITICAL LEADERS OF THE WORLD."

The funeral rites have been engraved on many of the medals. An Assassination Medal depicting the actual moment of assassination, with Governor and Mrs. Connally and the President and Mrs. Kennedy riding in the open limousine. In the background is the Dallas Schoolbook building. The assassin can be seen firing from the building. Running around the rim is the legend: "IN KENNEDY ABIECTA VIS DALLAS MCMLXIII."

From Canada comes a metallic memorial showing the Kennedy grave at Arlington with fence and Eternal Flame featured in the center. Its inscription says: "AND SO LET THE WORD GO FORTH THAT THE TORCH HAS BEEN LIT." Circumscribing this is a wreath of olive leaves, a few stars, and the President's name.

There are numerous medals of various designs and different coin value, metallic content, size, etc. One of the most dramatic is the Netherlands metallic issue called "Civil Rights Act of 1964." It was struck in honor of Martin Luther King, the Negro leader, and commemorated the passage of the Civil Rights Act of 1964 for which Kennedy fought so diligently. On the one side, one sees the stern visage of Martin Luther King superimposed on a motto from the Bible: "SO FAITH, HOPE, LOVE ABIDE, THESE THREE: BUT THE GREATEST OF THESE IS LOVE. I Corinthians 13:13, along with the name of the Negro leader. On the reverse side of the medal there appears the United States seal, the torch of Liberty, and the date on which the Civil Rights Act became law. The motto reads: "CIVIL RIGHTS ACT J. F. KENNEDY — L. B. JOHNSON ERA." On the right is the date: July 2, 1964.

Commemorative medals have been struck by countries around the world. The Dutch Peace Corps medal, honoring President Kennedy, has these

MEXICO

MEXICO

THE NETHERLANDS

SWITZERLAND

TAIWAN

TAIWAN

WEST GERMANY

WEST GERMANY

inscriptions: A NOBLE SERVANT OF PEACE and A MAN DOES WHAT HE MUST.

In June, 1964, the Austrian Ambassador to the United States, Dr. Wilfried Platzer, presented a gold medal representing the late President to Robert F. Kennedy, then Attorney General of the United States.

The Shiekdom of Sharjah has struck 33,000 5-rupee commemorative coins, plus 10,000 proofs of President Kennedy. They are sold in a plush box with a stamped-in portrait of the President.

A commemorative medallion has been issued by Germany; and a large, three-inch medallion has been struck in Switzerland. The Bavarian state mint's gold John F. Kennedy Memorial Medal was distributed on the first anniversary of the assassination.

Thus, on coin and medal, as in the hearts of people, the name of John F. Kennedy is forever inscribed.

WEST GERMANY

WEST GERMANY

THE JOHN F. KENNEDY
CENTER FOR THE PERFORMING ARTS

THE JOHN F. KENNEDY
CENTER FOR THE PERFORMING ARTS

CONTRIBUTIONS OF FOREIGN NATIONS

In September 1958, during the Eisenhower administration, Congress passed an act authorizing the creation of a national center for the performing arts in the nation's capital, to be named the National Cultural Center.

The need for a cultural center arose out of a number of considerations. First, the United States was the only leading country, and Washington the only major capital, which did not provide a national forum for the performing arts. Such a void made it seem that Americans were indifferent to the arts at a time when we wanted the world to know that our way of life does indeed provide the best environment for the spiritual and cultural development of mankind. Besides, talented newcomers had to seek training and experience overseas to win the recognition needed to join the ranks of our own distinguished artists. And despite the great increase in cultural activity everywhere, and the fact that Washington is one of the world's major centers, America did not bestow on her own performing artists the same national encouragement or acknowledgment given to statesmen, heroes, and scientists.

Soon after the assassination, a spontaneous movement arose throughout the country to make the Cultural Center, in which President Kennedy had taken personal interest, his sole official memorial in the nation's capital. President Johnson sent an administration request to Congress in December,

1963. The measure was passed with full bipartisan support, and on January 23, 1964, Lyndon Johnson signed the act in dedication of the Center, renaming it The John F. Kennedy Center for the Performing Arts. The President invited Senator Edward M. Kennedy to speak on behalf of the family at the signing ceremonies, and the younger brother of the President said: "This is something that was extremely close to the President's heart and to Jackie's heart as well. . ."

The original name was changed, but the aims and purposes remained the same: to serve all the people of the United States in providing long overdue national recognition of our great achievements in the performing arts; to give impetus to the artistic activities of local communities; to honor the art of other countries in a national setting. It was to be, in the words of President Johnson, "a living force for the encouragement of art."

The Center is charged with presenting the finest in the performing arts: in music, ballet, opera, musical theater, drama, and poetry. It is designed to establish stars and talented newcomers, national and international festivals, folk singing programs and lectures. It is to be charged also with encouraging and fostering the arts throughout the country, to bring the best in live entertainment to the people in their own communities. To this end, the Center has undertaken the joint sponsorship, with the Metropolitan Opera, of a national opera company. For the first time, the Center will provide a national setting for the presentation of distinguished performers from abroad.

Sources of the Center's audience will be some ten million annual visitors to the national capital; annual trips by thousands of children to Washington, the headquarters of more than eight hundred organizations; and America's two hundred million people will be part of the larger audience by means of the most modern communications system, including radio, television, tape recordings, and educational broadcasting.

Designed by architect Edward Durell Stone, the building consists of three halls under a single roof, with approximate seating capacities of 2,750 in the symphony hall, 1,150 in the theater, and 2,200 in the hall for opera, ballet, and musical theater. A garden-like roof area will be available for band concerts, art exhibits, festivals, children's theater, theater-in-the-round, halls and restaurants. The entire building will be sheathed in white marble facing,

John Fitzgerald Kennedy Center for the Performing Arts, Washington, D.C.

and will be surrounded by a series of delicate steel columns encased in bronze with a gold finish. The site, on the banks of the Potomac River, has been described by Mr. Stone as "one of the most exciting and glorious settings in the world for a public building."

A new model of the Center, 7 x 9 x 18 feet, built on a scale of 1/8th inch to one foot and made almost entirely of plastic, went on display on May 18, 1967. The model is electrically lit, enabling the viewer to see inside the Hall of Nations, the Hall of States, the Grand Foyer; and on the roof terrace level, the lobby of the Studio Playhouse, the Pavilion, the restaurant and cafeteria and the galleries. Model makers Alexander and Jones, of Huntington, Long Island, created the model which includes also surrounding landscape and the interior facilities.

The act creating the Center in 1958 provided also the land, but stipulated that funds for the building was to come from voluntary contributions of the American poeple. However, the 1964 act renaming the Center the John F. Kennedy Center provided for an appropriation of Federal funds to the extent of $15.5 million, to be matched by contributions from the public. On June 30, 1965, the Kennedy Center officials announced that public subscriptions had matched the requirements of the bill. More than 10,000 persons gave gifts ranging from mere pennies to $5 million from the Ford Foundation. Substantial donations in various amounts were received from many corporations, foundations, schools, and university students.

On December 2, 1964, President Johnson, before an audience of a thousand, including members of the Kennedy family, the diplomatic corps, the Supreme Court, and the Cabinet, lifting a historic spade which had been used to break ground for the Lincoln and Jefferson memorials, turned the earth on the Potomac River site, marking the official beginning of the construction program. He said:

> This Center will brighten the life of Washington. But it is not just a Washington project. It is a national project. It is a national project and a projection. It is important to know that the opportunity we give to the arts is a measure of the quality of our civilization. It is im-

portant to be aware that artistic activity can enrich the life of our people, which really is the central object of government.

President Kennedy had a deep sense of the importance of the arts. Artistic achievement was part of that pursuit of excellence which was his guiding star. It meant simply that each man should develop his own resources to the limit of his capacity, for his own fulfillment and for the benefit of his fellow men.

It was the role of government to liberate men for that pursuit. And it was also the role of government to share in recognition of their achievement.

He also recognized in art something that revealed enduring truths about human beings and their struggles.

Those truths would last and find an audience as long as civilization would last.

He knew that America would be judged, in large measure, on the basis of its artistic achievements as a mirror of the quality of our civilization.

President Kennedy was also a man who admired courage. And he saw in the artist an example of the rarest sort of courage; the courage to confront the world as it is and to search within yourself for the truth.

It is often far easier to immerse yourself in daily problems than to impose the solitary discipline and detachment necessary for creative work.

He believed this and respected it.

This Center is a tribute to those beliefs. It can be a center of imagination and energy for the entire nation.

Almost despite ourselves, we have become one of the cultural leaders of the world.

American performers and writers, painters and singers have led much of contemporary art and thought.

We are almost the last to recognize this enormous artistic surge.

This Center will serve as a reminder and as a continuing spur to our obligation to develop the vast cultural resources of American life.

St. Francis said: 'A single sunbeam is enough to drive away many shadows.'

President Kennedy proved this in his life.

The Kennedy Center will be another source of light.

The Fine Arts Accessions Committee of the Center has accepted the following:

A portrait of President Kennedy by Carlos Anderson, a gift of the artist.

A Steinway Grand Piano, a gift of Mrs. Edward Sloane.

A mural painting by Mark Rothko, a gift of Mrs. Albert Lasker.

A Japanese Byobu folding two-panel screen, a gift of Japanese women.

A recording of Enesco's first and second Rumanian rhapsodies conducted by the composer, a gift of Mr. Donald H. Gabor.

Seven foreign nations have made substantial contributions to enhance the beauty of the living memorial to President Kennedy:

Denmark has authorized a $155,000 gift of custom-made furniture for the Center's Grand Foyer, which is to be 600 feet long, 40 feet wide, and 60 feet high. The furnishings are designed by one of Denmark's leading architects, Poul Kjaerholm.

From Germany, the Center has received a gift of bronze doors for the main entrance, bearing two seals of the United States. The doors and seals are handcrafted by the leading German sculptor, Jurgen Weber. The gift has a value of $250,000.

The Republic of Ireland is presenting the Center with a Waterford chandelier. It has a value of $35,000 and will hang in the Presidential Reception Room on the box tier of the Opera House.

The Italian Government is donating 3,000 tons of white marble worth more than $1 million, for the entire Center. Former President Segni of Italy promised the gift to the late President Kennedy when he visited the country in June, 1963. The first shipment arrived in December 1966, and was formally presented by Ambassador Sergio Fenoultea. Quarrying of all the marble in the vicinity of Carrara has been completed. Some of it was taken from the same quarries which Michelangelo used for his statues. Three companies — Bufalini, Montecatini, and Henraux — are supplying the marble, which is being cut according to architectural specification before being crated for export. The American Export Isbrandtsen Lines will transport the marble at no cost to the Kennedy Center.

The Japanese Government and the American-Japan Society of Tokyo gave a magnificent red silk curtain, hand-woven with gold, which will hang from the proscenium of the Opera House. The Japanese Government will contribute the equivalent of $70,000 to the cost of the curtain, and a similar amount will be raised from private individuals and industry by the Society. Ceremonies of presentation were held in February, 1967, at which time Mr. Teruo Hachiya, Executive Director of the Society, presented the gift, unveiling a 50-inch-square sample of the curtain, which measures 47 by 117 feet. His Excellency Ryuji Takeuchi, Japan's Ambassador to the United States, presided. The design of the curtain, described as "springing flowers," symbolic of progress, to capture the New Frontier spirit of President Kennedy, was conceived by Mr. Shimura of Nishijin. Master Weaver Sasaki is directing the project.

Twelve crystal chandeliers were presented to the Concert Hall by the Norwegian Government, designed by Jonas Hidle and fabricated by the Christiania Glasmagasen, near Oslo. Value of the chandeliers is $180,000.

The Swedish Government, through its Ambassador Hubert de Besche, announced a contribution of fourteen crystal chandeliers, being fabricated by Orrefors Glassworks, Sweden. Designed by Carl Fagerbind, Orrefors' specialist in glass light fixtures, in coordination with the Kennedy Center's architect Edward Durell Stone, the chandeliers, worth over $200,000, will hang in the 630-foot-long Grand Foyer. They are made up of twelve graduated rows of hand-blown lead crystal double prisms. When the prisms are fully assembled, the frame of the chandeliers is not visible; light from any source is refracted in an arresting display of color. Each chandelier measures about 15 feet in length and 9 feet at the widest point, and weighs 7,000 pounds.

JOHN F. KENNEDY
CENTER FOR THE
PERFORMING ARTS

Many other countries have expressed their desire to present gifts to the Center. They are: Austria, Belgium, Canada, Czechoslovakia, France, Great Britain, Iran, Kuwait, Portugal, and Spain.

Thus, the nations of the world, paying homage to John F. Kennedy in yet another manifestation, express agreement with the President's assertion that " in the fulfillment. . .of. . .responsibilities toward the arts lies our unique achievement as a free society."

Goldman
John Fitzgerald Kennedy